The National Poetry Review
Issue Number Eight

Winter 2008

Editor:
C. J. Sage

Subscriptions:

Individuals: $12 per year
Institutions: $18 per year
(Please add sufficient postage amount for first class or air mail outside the United States)

**TNPR reads magazine submissions in email only. Please see website for guidelines.**

Address **subscriptions** to:

C. J. Sage, Editor
*The National Poetry Review*
Post Office Box 2080
Aptos, California 95001-2080

For prize offerings and submissions guidelines, please visit
www.nationalpoetryreview.com

The National Poetry Review is a 501 (c) (3) non-profit organization.

*The National Poetry Review* is distributed in the United States and Canada by Ingram Periodicals, and indexed by *Humanities International Complete* and *The Index to American Periodical Verse*.

The National Poetry Review Copyright 2003, 2004, 2005, 2006, 2007, 2008, 2009
All rights reserved
ISBN 978-0-9821155-2-7
ISSN 1543-3455

Cover Art: "Believing in It" by Lynne Taetzsch
www.artbylt.com

## Poetry

| | |
|---|---|
| Mia Nussbaum: *My Wife Was Gone; It Startles* | 5 |
| Sam Byfield: *The Itch* | 9 |
| Martha Zweig: *Mr. Bluster Housesits; Rebirthday* | 11 |
| Sarah Blackman: *The _____ Impossible* | 15 |
| Amit Majmudar: *The Art of Tesselation* | 18 |
| Angie Estes: *Alleluya* | 21 |
| Darren Morris: *Early Thaw : The Vessel Called Our Bodies : : Salvation :* | 23 |
| Jeanette Allee: *Through the Skeletoned Air* | 26 |
| Oliver de la Paz: *Self-Portrait with Taxidermy; How I Learned Quiet* | 27 |
| Beth Martinelli: *Poem without Rain or the Sea* | 31 |
| T. Zachary Cotler: *Painted Ballad of the Ore Train Daughter; Waysong...* | 33 |
| Patrick Carrington: *That Place Where Everything Goes* | 48 |
| Mark Conway: *necropolitan* | 50 |
| Teresea Chuc Dowell: *L'art D'aimer* | 52 |
| Ben Berman: *Footing and the Solid Ground; Before You; Quicksand* | 53 |
| Dyani Johns: *1352 Lighthouse Way* | 61 |
| Melissa Stein: *New Dominion* | 63 |
| Rita Mae Reese: *At the Castillo de San Marcos* | 65 |
| Cindy Beebe: *What Happens Next* | 70 |
| Angela Vogel: *Flower Bed* | 72 |
| J. P. Dancing Bear: *Legitimacy Is So Chummy; Magic, It Is; Deadline World* | 74 |
| Dorianne Laux: *Dog Moon* | 79 |
| Lee Upton: *Dear Succubus* | 81 |
| Lesley Wheeler: *The Unbeliever Takes a Hike* | 83 |

## Essays & Interviews

| | |
|---|---|
| Judith Harris: A Study of Ted Kooser's "Etude" | 85 |
| Tony Leuzzi: An Interview with Karen Volkman | 90 |
| **Notes on the Authors** | 102 |

Mia Nussbaum

## *My Wife Was Gone*

And when I woke

my wife was gone.

That day was not like the day

I saw an elephant, festooned

and strung with bells

idling in a dusty town.

Not like a day

in which bloomed

julep cups, sheet cake.

A leak began on my left side.

I commenced to unbutton

my wrists. I commenced to forget

the acts of her tongue.

Her leaven and holidays.

Marcelled rows of trees

receded. And with them

went such quiet. I missed

the horse-like creatures,

four meters high.

The long stretches

# Mia Nussbaum

of uninhabitable ice.

I missed the sounds of the seas

when the seas were whales

and the time when I was not.

We had been gatherers

of nightshade in the brief epochs

of nightshade. Now it was charging

in trucks. This was not Bismark,

but us. So surrounded

and entirely alone, I averred I was

no variety of gangster

and let the roof forge down.

Mia Nussbaum

## *It Startles*

Who can punctuate it? Wife.

The unplantable blacktops in the past

of my wife. The hurricaned

petals. The combustible joints

of wife. My wife getting naked

under stars in a car.

The chiseled and serif typeface

of wife. The radiance:

her fancies and goodnights.

Natural law's deduced from such

movements. In the house whose root

is my life. Dusky,

sometimes a lioness

sleeping. Taking dictation

for briefs. Courting in malls

gone to seed. What astonishes.

Who? Cur'rants, coop'ers, wife.

For'bear'ance, for bear ance, life.

We refused the agents

of mansionization, my wife.

# Mia Nussbaum

We put the palm chakras

over the eyes, which eat light.

Yet we never rolled a rug

and played a gramophone.

And we never bit the sugar knuckle

to the sugar bone.

Wife, you say you saw

the hook and carcass

swing in the door.

Tell how we took a bus to the beach

to watch the cook fires go. The waves

were mushy, the dark

fettered down. Are pictographs

better? Is archness the answer?

Bonny. Ennui. To do it

without the assistance of machines.

Among pleas. For a time, wife and I,

we were festively clothed. The flung,

stony planets made wishes on us.

Blinking wife, thinking wife, my piebald

stitched, my soldered life.

Now! The cold! Is! Past!

Sam Byfield

## *The Itch*

I thought it might have been a mozzie

but it wasn't, and I lost a sock.

The sofa keeps its secrets like a rock.


Too early in the Spring for mosquitos

but not for spiders. Last night

I heard them clomping around in the roof


in stilettos, then doing the sort of waltz

you only see in town-halls and on tv.

Out here past the suburbs when lights go


out, the slow weave crawl of satellites

between stars, down into the mountains

through trapdoors. I saw a comet, though


it wailed like an ambulance and carried

the injured. The pie shop's started closing

early on the weekend to the complaints

and short-term malnutrition of bachelors.

The dog has worms and barks at other dogs.

A cat approached the front door, didn't stay.

All the appliances hummed in the cat's

absence. Moths lit fires in the sky.

I wore a hat and thought about pies.

Martha Zweig

## Mr. Bluster Housesits

Trot the dog along the whistling graveyard.

Humor the dog of the lady who's Not Home,

but whose neighborhood's also Not Famine & Not War

all day long.


All roads range & return. The dog

fetches in such delight the keys you tossed you toss

the keys again, & then in your unguarded

instant stooped at the lady's door the dog

sticks a sloppy tongue in your ear.


Drunk disease has that lived-in look, shape of the couch.

The TV fumbles among remotes, finds whatever it wants

until you want whatever it finds: species reportedly

local to the body hair in hovels, tracks of international


infant tears, but keep

your cheeks to yourself & hands to thy service,

o distant Lord whose overseers

visit to overlook.

# Martha Zweig

The dog kibbles, the dog resettles a round bed that it likes.

Not the dog's soul, then, scratching: nip in the air,

whines to get out, catching a fleet scent of itself on the ill

wind blowing the no-good

up & away & head-over-heels with the pro-

&-con man. Huff puff, the con man breathes.

The house staggers up & down.

Martha Zweig

## *Rebirthday*

Lucky day lottery: I post

my entry wherever law prohibits the void.

Say I submit my 25

good deeds or less, each to its brown parcel

pending reappraisal. What more

(I contend) could a normal person need?


Heroics: I started the day breathing, mouth-to-mouth.

Welcome back to the calendar! Recovery

assigns its rooms first-come,

occupants subject to random


locker-check & confiscation of items. Install, please, a few

fewer urgent engagements in a more orderly manner.


Wet gray lunch tray: today I favor the house loaf &

mushroom gravy. I used to like appetite best illicit

in a vinyl booth, next to the local wordsmith with a little

smoky alcohol; I liked the burning-cold

sopping cotton swab he helped me to,

# Martha Zweig

then puncture & plunger, ah,

but, as I was just about-to-be saying,

the mind I meant to speak tonight taught heart-to-heart

an antic you need to know. Just try: your second wind

won't snuffle any of those candles out.

Every wicked fizzle reignites. Next-

to-last gasp you won't even wish.

*Winner of The Laureate Prize for Poetry*

Sarah Blackman

*The _____ Impossible*

Agreed. I am alone, solving this historical

drama in another Alabama summer. What

did you do today, and you say: The shopping.


It wasn't sexy when heat came up

through the floor boards. I rolled in cotton

panties to stay cool and the neighbor kids dug


again into your planter, turned the buckles

of stone to grub the roots. A ruddy bouquet

to tie to handlebars and race with. Your peonies,


your struggling Solomon's seal. There are clues:

the motorcade of searchers, a psychic's dream of the dark tree.

And what about the shed behind the house?


What about its floors—oiled dirt and stain proof?

After the fire—only in the one room—

and the second newscast that made her mother look

# Sarah Blackman

fatter and more unsure, I took again to the porch

swing where I can push with the ball of my foot

and startle, predictably, the wren.

*Come Back Shae Shae* is iced on the rear window

of your neighbor's boyfriend's car. I think he's

for the oldest two, you say, the little ones are light.

And that girl too—last seen a red head, a pink shirt,

those blue shoes, the school bus—has gone to Florida.

Sometimes, they will steal the children

for their organs, put hearts and kidneys in buckets

of ice like cod. A mother here will lose

her daughter to the pavement, the knots in her shoestrings,

the levels of burden—panic, fire, slogans

on the neighbor's lawn, or quiet—and in the mornings,

I will leave your house too slowly to have ever been there.

Last night I said, I'm leaving and made it to the living

room. In the dark, with one shoe still in my hand. What did you do today, and you say: I already said I love you.

Amit Majmudar

## *The Art of Tesselation*

1.

When Escher emerged from the Alhambra, flocks

Interlocked overhead, migrating

In opposite directions, both directions south.

The plane tilted, and the spaces between birds

Turned into fish and populated seas.

The tiles came alive. Taxonomy

Softened their diamonds into feline eyes

Fluorescing with the Fiat lux's flashlight

That stopped him in the Garden. Who goes there?

A goateed Dutchman, with no formal training

In mathematics; a draughtsman, showing us

A stage intermediate between matter

And spirit, the sterile Plane seminally split,

Quickened first with symmetry and then with life.

2.

His eschatology was reassuring: Death must be

A staircase down to a breezy rooftop, a whole house

Of antigravity staircases where souls

Amit Majmudar

Hurry their millipede legs toward God.

How often he divided the Plane into opposites

Buttressing each other: the batwinged squatnecked imp

And the Renaissance seraph, the hunchbacked

Eschar-black gargoyle and the upright man

Who circle out of their common plane to shake hands.

The famous hands that draw each other

Answer the hands in the Sistine Chapel.

Between those index fingers, creation

Lightningbolts all one way, not one salmon

Of imagination thrashing upstream.

Here, one hand is Adam's, one is God's; no one,

Least of all Escher, can say which is which.


3.

Nothing's so mystical as symmetry,

Except, I think, the way asymmetry

Can be transfigured into symmetry

By repetition. The kaleidoscope

Is proof that God does not play dice. You can

Make anything sound predetermined just

By rhyming on it twice. Symmetry may

# Amit Majmudar

Be pretty, but asymmetry identifies:

The victim's body by a mole, her killer

By his lazy eye.

Angie Estes

## *Alleluya*

Abundant in woods and shady

places, it flowers between Easter

and Whitsuntide and is also called

Cuckoos' meat *by reason when it springeth*

*forth and flowereth the Cuckoo singeth most,*

*at which time also Alleluya was wont*

*to be sung in churches*: five white

petals, veined with purple. In Fra Angelico's

altarpiece painting of the Annunication,

the Archangel hails Mary and ducks

as the white dove of the Holy Spirit slides

out of God's hand on a golden beam

straight into Mary's heart. Beyond

    the portico, outside in the Garden, Adam

    and Eve lean together while *Alleluya*

    springs up in each place their feet have

    touched because it was believed

    that *Ave* could walk backwards to undo

    the sin of *Eva* in the same way that sign

# Angie Estes

                    can play leapfrog with sing. According to

                  a fifteenth-century botanical glossary,

                *Alleluya herba habens tria folia et r*

              with a halo above the *r*, a sign

            which can stand for *recto, regio,*

          *ratio,* or *responsio*: An upright

        plant—a region, a reckoning,

response—*Alleluya*

sends up thin leaves, each composed

of three heart-shaped leaflets,

bright above but purple

underneath, and only in shade

are they fully extended: the direct

rays of the sun cause them

to sink into a pyramid

on the stem, and at night

or in rough weather the leaflets fold

their hearts in half

and hold them

side by side.

# Darren Morris

## *Early Thaw : The Vessel Called Our Bodies : : Salvation :*

I have the doe by the ears,

and my friends have me by a rope

knotted at my waist. I have crawled

to her on my belly like some predator.

On the banks, they have bent the rope

round a little tree to leverage muscle

against this thawing pond.

I hold her head to my own.

Her breath, a bleating fire.

Her quick bark, a cuss—a briar

for the sleetfall's tiny hammers—

tapering off as the heart must

when it begins to freeze.

And now she must know

I mean her no harm but the kind

of salvation which is my own.

She must know that she will

become every woman

I ever love, just as she must

know we are only boys

# Darren Morris

and will not be strong enough

to pull her out—as I too

must know, but do not believe.

For I hold her life to mine.

For her eyes are in me still, and

the real thing of one blind

hoof is on the surface pawing

for some solid stance

the way she did when she was born,

shaking off the silence of that

white-cold dope into this

measured being. But she will not

stand again, and the weight of her

begins to slip my grasp as the fight

in her recedes. Still I hold her

behind the small prongs that

she wears like a tiara. I love her,

and I will find no other, though she

is vanishing with the rest to some place

the body does not belong. No vessel for

her sweetnesses or for her swift,

sure flights between the trees

that made her myth and kept her alive.

Darren Morris

I want to know her more and will not

let her go. I want to suspend her

till the spring, put air back in her

glassy lungs, and swim her

to the shore. This dreaming is what

breaks in boys as it does in ice.

It cracks us open, swallowing

whole, the doe in my full

embrace, the rope tether trailing

from my tenders. Now we are weightless.

Our graceless struggle loosed. Nearly

all of what the body means, sloughed,

save my cheek upon her muzzle,

my fingers on her cello's neck.

Now we spin in absent time

like the final dancers at the prom,

so slowly that the lights turn down

around us. And just before we kiss,

high above, with our final breath,

my friends—I thought had given in—

are pulled straight through, one by one,

the blazing hole in the broken ice.

Jeanette Alée

## Through the Skeletoned Air

If someone could kindly shoot me
out of a cannon
              ball into the next life

    past cellphone slatterns
    smutty grafitti
    prime rib raised on beer and pornography
    federal long distance
    excise fees

Release me like a Flying Wallenda
in a freshly washed pair of tights

*You stop me midair to ask, do I fear death?*
*—I know I have a skeleton inside me*
*with plans to eventually get some fresh air, still—*

I want to be winging towards that place
where every banana could be answered like a telephone
Towards your open arms, your open
Honey, can you put the newspaper down?
Honey, I think I'm headed,
I think I'm absolutely headed

Oliver de la Paz

## Self-Portrait with Taxidermy

In my anatomy studies, I expected
fetal pigs, the pink bodies flush
against plastic in a swirl of formaldehyde.

The lacquered workbenches of the lab
and the light from the fluorescents
made us all ghoulish with our tools.

I was ready to live with the smell,
to pin back the skin with the packet of pins
and the scalpels we were given.

Instead, the teacher pulled, from a refrigerator,
six pheasants he bagged
on a weekend excursion to the sage desert.

Our disappointment hung in our faces, but
we shucked it off. The smell of the body cavities
and blood was an interminable horizon.

A bucket of baking soda between us all,
we had to skin the things yet be gentle enough
to keep their skins intact. I settled in,

the dissection pans turned white from the powder
with drizzles of some unguent, something none of us
had ever witnessed. An occasional bead

clanged on my pan. My body was riddled

# Oliver de la Paz

with buckshot. I wondered if I'd be able
to salvage even the idea of pheasant.

I too had killed a bird, a headshot
from several yards earlier in the year. The loon jerked
then folded like a napkin, its neck

sagging like stems from a cut flower.
No one saw me fire the gun, even though the shot
thundered long after. That late afternoon

I had felt volcanic. The clouds came and went,
everything sputtered . . . candle-sure,
the way the color of childhood was meant to be.

The body of a loon rippled some distance.
It would soon wash ashore. I was praying
the lake wouldn't forsake me, utterly.

And when its form rolled up the bank, I was quick
to bury it, lest my father know that I had played
with the rifle and in my play, I had broken.

There is so much that clings to us, the licking sound
of the lake, the glint of a scalpel catching the green
aurorae from the humming fixtures.

The susurrations of our compressed breathing
was boundless. We were awaiting some deliverance
from our gory task. The V of a rifle sight

dipped true into afternoon biology. Our knives

Oliver de la Paz

rose and fell and we quickly scooped the white powder
into the wounds we made.

The pheasants were surely things that would call to us,
to choose us.  For, one by one we are called
to make something ready.  To give back form

and put everything back in its place.

Oliver de la Paz

*How I Learned Quiet*

Begin with slowness—the drag of a candle's flame

down to the guard, and the pump of blood into the heart

as it sinks in the ribcage. Everything was spectacle.

Mother pinched me for squirming. The timetables lied. The games

were un-winnable. The priest looked down upon me

and lo, I was a fidgeting thing. God was in the desert

feeding me cactus flowers and locusts. I sank

my cheek between my teeth and listened

to the helicopters above us. Someone coughed. Someone

held up their hands and let fabric slide down to his elbows.

*Winner of The Finch Prize for Poetry (Larissa Szpoluk, judge)*

Beth Martinelli

## Poem Without Rain or the Sea

I think it is real, the ruby eyes of pond rats,

stolen swan hearts bloodied and still beating.

Growls inside the radiator, a girl, black curls,

her silence as her brother slices shadows

back from bodies. They fall away like mosaics

of dark ice when a river warms then closes over.

In the dolls' saucers he serves them: rainy

platefuls of blackbird pie. Through a window

the moon is a spindle; night cranks its cold wheel.

This night bears no comparisons; loose sky

shakes and sputters. Spiders falling. They circle

and weave. There is danger in happiness,

a nest of goblins with a whole bag of tricks.

Ants take the shoebox attic beam by beam.

The doll corpse moves thin lips underground:

# Beth Martinelli

*Speak the names of fallen cities.* A smooth, paint-brushed groom ashamed of his bride. Matchstick chalkboard, the equation wrong: x not equal to absence.

The miniature parlor, deserted chintz. Winter's sunset again clotting. A hired man carries a cider press through the dry gardens; invisible birds mute their songs.

*2nd & 3rd Place in the Finch Prize for Poetry, both by:*

T. Zachary Cotler

## Painted Ballad of the Ore Train Daughter

*For two voices (tenor; baritone in italics), banjo, housepaint can, and upright bass.*

*Verse of the Worm:*

The town she came to,

being born, was a ring

of squares and wicker

chairs, and corn, green,

gritty corn. She bit

the tit the sisters gave her

at the temple by the fields,

good sickle-hammer fields,

good yields each

year but the year

she was born,

and the men stood

## T. Zachary Cotler

medium-sized around

the freak of her

nativity: her thicker hair

and outland beak.

Those men talked black

and bluestreaks through

the morning— who

her father was, not one

of them, *could never be*,

he must have come

in on an ore train,

autumn, in a storm.

Out back, a thresher

split in two a worm

T. Zachary Cotler

with skin the many

petal-hues of cyclamen,

and the half-worms grew

and curled off through

the corn,

the morning

she was born,

*being born.*


*Verse of the Name:*


When she was nine,

chalk-doodling on

the warped sienna

highwayside, a sister pulled

alongside in a poultry

# T. Zachary Cotler

truck and plucked a name

out of the Book of Ur-tarnation —

get inside this truck and be

called *do not speak,* the ballad

singer sang aside, *speak not*

*the gun damned name,*

*for so to speak will*

*Greek-to-me the daughter's dun*

*clay and the banjo-twang*

*my families call salvation* and we will

drive, said the sister, to the filling

station, central on this

railroad nation, by the place

where you got born,

*being born.*

T. Zachary Cotler

*Verse of the Filling Station:*

Now the sister pumped the oil,

meanwhile, the daughter chalked

cave figures on the truck dash —

dry-heat lightning, oriental, lashed

the fields, and the pump balked.

In the town, the men stood

ringwise, steak-jawed men

bluespeaking not of course

about the daughter, or whose

goodwife chopped a sauerkraut

damned-Sodom fine or coarse,

also the township, too

few crewmen on the corn

seas, and a darker season

T. Zachary Cotler

slamming in the power-

wire rigging. And the pump

unbalked as the sister knocked

the nozzle on the truck—

oil sprew in a lady's fan

shape out a notch-eyed flue,

and two mechanics stubbed

their cigarettes out in their hats.

The daughter gaffed a brush

out of the soapbucket and drew

self-portraits abstract in the stain,

each head a fossil sun, each hair

a soap-and-darker coil,

good oil to shape in,

in the lightning

quiet of the filling

station, just beyond

the town's imagination.

*Verse of her Virginity:*

She was a buxom one,

bright dun. She was

a twisting in the corn,

and he came, man and shadow

man, along the half-paths

of the worm that'd twinned

the morning she was

born. He came together

with a hatbrim-tipping,

T. Zachary Cotler

    mezzotinted in the morning,

    morn. She did not have to
    be at school for half-an-hour

    yet, good pennycopper
    buttons popping off a silk-husk

    blouse, and more. She did
    not have to, yet she did it

    twisting, man and shadow
    shock, man to her ore, hysteric

    core. One train,
    rocking by beyond

    the fields of her immunity
    to anything she never

    could adore,
    being torn.

T. Zachary Cotler

*Verse of the Dead Babe:*

This babe, so petal-hued

and fine, so few months

old inside, out of her body

came to rifle Satan's fold,

dead bold, *approximately dead*

at daybreak in the bed of her

recovery, the sisters hovering

black like birds of omen;

and the babe, it keened

syllabic and articulate almost.

A pancreatic blood attack,

the blood-dun irises tipped

back into her baby's head,

and on those iris trains

T. Zachary Cotler

she fled into the babe-head

of her aetiology, her own:

the temple and the worm corn

sown, the stormy

hood of Azrael thrown

upon where she was born,

and where she gave birth,

in the house of the sisters.

*Verse of Her Madnesses:*

She fricasseed an almanac

with tarragon and salt,

sent loveletters to leaders

of the Necro-onom-ikon cult.

T. Zachary Cotler

She talked to etchings

in the sidewalk; they talked back,

those ones and minus-ones

along the cracks

— *best you get drunk*

*and buy a gun, girl,*

*you're a fine cornwhiskey*

*girl, with an intestine of a swine*

*strung on your fishing line,*

*and not a lake for miles,*

for miles, they said, *you*

*smile like Satan in his blood-blue*

*wine. Get drunk and find*

*the townsmen in their homes,*

*and make them dead,*

T. Zachary Cotler

the etchings said.

She fled into the sisters' house

instead, and read the Book.

*Verse of the Gun:*

When she was ninety-nine,

and her blood slipped thin

like turpentine, the town had spread

across the tracks, with smokestacks

tall as cowhorns of a God

and college quads and galleries.

She bought a gun and licensed it,

and bought some lead

and loaded it. The sun

clocked on the only hill, one

T. Zachary Cotler

inch above a ghostmeal mill,

*the sun. And nearly everyone* in need

of slaughter had demised of age or

been killed in a war before

the ore train daughter thought

to say her name aloud. The ballad

singer twanged and sang

to drown the sound — *to*

*shoot the one who thought her*

*up and say her name*

that he didn't write down, were

parallel actions, two lines meet —

and the singer could not

duck that yellow-white impasto

# T. Zachary Cotler

    shot along the south-to-

    north meridian of the cargo

    highway that had split

    the temple from the corn,

    beggared the rails that once fed

    men and metal to the town,

    wherein she had been born,

    being born.

## T. Zachary Cotler

## Waysong of the Hourglass Flipping

Not every end

is a goal. There is

Eve and Adam,

and their melody

ends, no goal, yet not

until ending did it

find its goal, so

I drip my wrists

across their glyphs. This

place is writ of what

I mean behind a veil when I

incant the humankind

who walked and fell

here, too — they bit the wrists

of masterminded angels,

flung mysterium, mysterium,

and fucked as blossoms. Falling

here is outbreak, here

is my trapdoorway down

to heaven ground.

Patrick Carrington

## *That Place Where Everything Goes*

The life I lead inside my head is nothing

like the one out here. It's cushy;

if it were female I'd need to make babies with it

right away. You will not find the gritted smile I smile

when I'm trying not to scream or me leading

with my chin. Getting back on my feet

every morning does not take character.

The trick is turning all this into a story you can like.

I like having another world to hold

my missing laundry socks, where it's okay

to pick up hitchhikers, to hit an inside straight.

No one thinks I'm crazy when I move the checkers

in the back row and I'm not shot at like a gamebird

if I happen to say *God* in a classroom or *evolution* in church.

I'm forgiven for all the things I think on bad nights,

can forget the questions I ask when I'm alone,

the faces I see on the ceiling, that sick

feeling in the pit of my stomach.

The last breath of each day is not the soft,

whizzing sound of a spent rocket—

## Patrick Carrington

In this other place always I am faithful,

I have never been cruel. I do not produce

any category of garbage that speaks

more eloquently about me than I ever could myself.

I am more than what I throw away. I am not there

to be used up. And when all else fails, I raise my face

to the rain. It feels good and clean. Time stops

and I'm the only one there, far away and safe

behind a curtain I never examine too closely.

# Mark Conway

## *necropolitan*

the sun is real, but lies.

librarians re-informed us

we'd been warned. but

who reads schiller anymore?

all the excess visions had

been booked. the best

are overloved. the river runs

through dinkytown, accepting

all its slops. the town fish live,

celebrities, scavenging on chemicals

and tripe, what they eat helps them

eat up what they eat, sweet

genetic engineering. We posit

they prefer this rise in appetite.

                                      any-

more, there are no visions, no

visors, neither, nor sun screen

needed to block the once-

anticipated vision burn.

shit mon petit, there simply isn't

Mark Conway

time, the sun runs like honey

through the molten hive.

they say the over-honeyed

occupants hate licking

lilacs twice.  the sun is real

but lies.  you stop time

by simply ceasing breathing,

death is how you see

behind, the way you know

someone is back there

when that certain someone

stares.

## Teresa Chuc Dowell

### L'art D'aimer

*from the perspective of Baltimore Orioles*

First are the songs— a composition of whistles

and rattles. *You always hear an oriole before*

*you see one.* Then copulation; black and

orange ruffles in leaves. They find a branch high

above the ground to weave a bag. Pieces of plastic strips,

strings, branches, grass, one by one in the beak,

mixes with saliva. In the building and in its intent

is nest and what is to come afterwards — eggs,

hatchlings helpless and blind, throats stretched

out in a choral for food. Insect legs dangle

from a parent's beak. The younglings will soon leave

the nest with a nudge off the edge — the first time

wings are used to convince air of its ability.

Between two elm trunks vertical and black —

bird in sky is an absolute.

Orioles migrate in the night air, navigating by

way of the stars, giving themselves entirely

to open spaces.

Ben Berman

## *Footing and the Solid Ground*

Between swigs of beer, Muvhenge would speed

after the rabbits hopping through the headlights.

Holly began crossing herself vigorously, so I

yelled up, *shaz, usatiuraye.* Muvhenge laughed

and without looking over said, *why would I*

*want to kill you? There's already one dead*

*body in the back.* I said, *there's a dead body*

*in the back?* and then Holly repeated, there's

a dead body in the back? and then we both

realized the bench we were sitting on

was a coffin. It was silent for a while

after that, other than the occasional swerve

and accompanying thud. Even the hills

had turned quiet, no signs of life anywhere

until we passed a bottle store and stopped

for one-one. I'd sipped mine halfway

and was declining advances from a heavy-

set woman when Muvhenge whistled

for us to leave. It was strange climbing back

into the car, having tasted the Pierian Spring.

# Ben Berman

Soon, the dirt road trailed off into a loose

landscape and we bouldered uphill over

mudstone and saplings. The car was

the only thing, that night, without shocks.

Jarring and slow going as it was, though,

at least we were staggering forward, unlike

when the path plateaued to cracked clay

and leaking wells and we found ourselves

mired in the muck. *Much of what happened*

*in Africa,* wrote Paul Theroux, *was not*

*tragedy but farce.* And here I was, stuck

in the mud with a cop, a corpse

and a born-again Christian. We searched

the area for slates or planks, anything

that might provide traction and grip.

We found stones, wedged them beneath

the wheels. Holly and I leaned on

the bumper as hard as we could, but we

were far from footing and the solid ground.

And the more we tried to push our way out,

the more we rocked ourselves deeper in.

Ben Berman

*Before You*

Before you, love always felt like

some drunk man beating at my hut,

begging me to pay dowry for the girl

he knocked up, who, having

shamed her family, sat shivering

beneath a blanket on her knees.

At most, I'd offer pliers,

a flash light, yesterday's rice —

none of which was ever enough,

but I figured things that show up

at your door are someone else's

problem. Besides, I didn't want

to negotiate love, I wanted the ground

to cave in. I wanted to tumble

with the crumbling

# Ben Berman

rock into a swirling sea of muck.

Though, having later fallen

into such a viscous ooze,

I discovered what happens

once we climb out— we get arrested

for picnicking on the grass, and even if

we argue a valid point (there were no signs)

we realize that being right is irrelevant

because this is about power (*we can't tell you*

*everything*), compromise and ultimately

the American dollar. A woman once left me

for that dollar, told me I'd never support

a certain lifestyle then ditched me like

an exotic pet that's grown too big to keep.

I was so desperate for reassurance

after that, so willing to shoehorn love

into a pressing fit and limping gait,

Ben Berman

I could have sneezed

right as some woman was bouncing

on top of me and wouldn't have

recoiled at the sudden awkwardness

of her breasts flopping about.

I was convinced intimacy,

or what passes for intimacy,

would redeem the sudden flop

of my life and it wasn't until

I was out walking one night

and a man dropped his pants

and began humping the intercom

beneath two glorious golden arches

that I remembered the night

is filled with delicious laughter,

that I allowed myself to imagine

# Ben Berman

a pubescent voice asking —

do you want fries with that?

And though the sweet arrival

and summity view may still be

awhile away, I'm trying to explain

that before you, love always felt

like a dead cat sprawled stiff

on someone else's driveway,

two other cats pawing at it

as I ran by.  But you showed up

like an abandoned balled up litter

of new-born kittens. And I'm ready

to reach in, peel the dead off

from the ones still gnawing.

Ben Berman

## Quicksand

Even if we have a landscape

    to return to — not just some

setting peppered with baobabs


and thatch-roofed huts, but one

    that speaks to experience

itself — a dried-out river, say,


and the bank collapsing

    beneath our feet,

and even if we fell into


that groundless ground,

    found ourselves suspended

between a float and sink,


still,


we can't escape the unheroic

    rescue (friend, walking

# Ben Berman

    stick) and how quickly

       afterwards do we forget

          our tentative measures,

    sink into a sure-footed

       rhythm, the pitfalls

         of solid ground

    growing more dangerous

       with every secure step.

Dyani Johns

## *1352 Lighthouse Way*

It came crashing down, the eiders

watching passively over their long

bills. They rose and fell on the

waves, saw only half of the collapse—

a house, small, ancient, its siding

eaten by salt on the wind, eaves

once proud, now arriving at

the slip-face of the dune. Over,

down into the trough. The eiders

dove, ducked their heads, rubbed

their smooth bodies with salt. On

the next crest, they saw timbers

jutting at odd angles, a beam

piercing the roof like a broken

femur burst through the muscle.

# Dyani Johns

Only the eiders heard the crack

and crash as the wind hurried

along what would come in time.

What they witnessed could not

have been more interesting than

the slim, silvery fish darting below.

Melissa Stein

## New Dominion

The pond breathes out the seclusion of another afternoon

unvisited by bodies. Everything is quiet but ugly—

not in the sense of its banks heaped

in decaying muck or sodden sportsocks,

but more like the leathered faces of the farmers

in those DPW photos from the Depression.

They didn't look resigned, exactly—just didn't know

there were alternatives, so realness shined out of them.

It's always seemed odd to me that at the vanishing point

of ugliness lies its opposite, that euphoria's tenor

is that of despair. Maybe we are limited in our truths,

and Ecclesiastes had it right. Maybe the sun

ringing this pond and its black collar of trees

is the one bad habit I don't have to unlearn.

The *kop-plunk* of some silly fish calls attention to itself

and it's the suspicious hard look of an eye toward the camera,

hard but carrying light, while the better-off are roving about

with their flashing gadgets and fancy suits, puffing

and sweaty and coffined in corn-dust. I promise myself

not to translate this pond, to let it be, downtrodden

Melissa Stein

and junk-filled but at least what it's always been.

Scummy surface traversed by waterbugs,

the clots of mosquitoes, tangly jungle of weeds

and rotting vines. It has no aspirations. It's a relief.

Rita Mae Reese

## *At the Castillo de San Marcos*

In front of one of the watchtowers,

   a plaque informs me:

"The builders were human."


And I wonder what they became.

   I think of what I have built,

not much—houses of Lincoln logs


or Legos or cards. A fence

   and a back porch, once,

long ago. I still feel, at times,


the swing of the hammer, the insisting sun

   of midday,

the coarse song of nails driven home.


A man once said that the soul is fastened,

   as if by a nail,

to the body. But it is fastened

# Rita Mae Reese

by countless nails, and every day more;

   there is no relief.

What have they built?


The walls of this fort are made

   not of wood but coquina—

thousands of tiny shells. The builders


were human: slaves, Timucuans,

   and convicts

whom the Spanish employed for 20¢ a day


—if the records are reliable—

   to erect this nearly invincible

fortress on the bay, protecting treasure ships


from pirates and foreign privateers.

   The Spanish sack,

the Germans plunder, the French pillage,


the Swedes and Danes ransack, and nearly everyone

   marauds. The Timucuans,

Rita Mae Reese

the previous residents of what is now

the state of Florida, built things from wood—

   part of the reason

so little of their culture has survived: a few artifacts,

a few words. For instance, seven words

   for *now*. Were they

possessed of a sense of Zen or urgency

(or some magical combination of both)?

   Did they create with wood

from a loyalty to the present,

wanting nothing they built to survive

   too long?

*Build* comes from Middle English

and meant "to construct a dwelling"

   and "to dwell,

as in an abode." From its origins,

# Rita Mae Reese

*build* needs only an *i*, but the *u*

   is nestled beside

—a cistern to catch rainwater,

a cup that will one day overflow.

   I make my home

in this world, and dwell here. Until.

Paradise, if we are to believe its origins,

   needs a wall.

So do prisons, forts, houses. But there might be

something that does not love it. God, maybe.

   *Get out. Do good works.*

The Castillo de San Marcos took 23 years to build.

Some time into its construction, an engineer

   informed the builders

their wall was three feet too low.

The builders were human.

   Perhaps this

Rita Mae Reese

is the same problem

the first lovers, God's thieving sharecroppers,
   encountered
with their garden wall. And, instead of warning them,

their Engineer pointed out other flaws and evicted.
   The builders were only human;
what recourse did they have?

Their wall was always too low
   or too high. The house
that you and I shared is vacant now.

The fence is gone, but the porch still stands.
   In the end, we had to evict ourselves,
pointing our god-stiff fingers before

jumping the wall and striking out on our own.

# Cindy Beebe

## *What Happens Next*

Have you heard? Tests have been done, it's one
       phantasmagorical and
  euphorically massive
          dot-to-dot.
                 Girl hooks
to llama hooks
to the little man in the top
hat and then you put the elephant
    plant between

the sea and a star. Are you ready now?
   Are you ready for stars
everywhere, sprouting, new shoots all over,

no more of this
wondering what they are.

      Elephant leaves twinkle.
The sea grows roots, and you, you flow
like water over the whistling rocks

_____ Cindy Beebe

             and the waking up rocks


and the fishes say, *sum es sumus*

and you realize no language

    ever dies


    and where's the island now, you ask

and everyone forgets

                how it felt

Angela Vogel

## Flower Bed

I marched the little query to the woods, plied it unspeakably,

it plopped down fast as nature forms a canopy,

it pulled out *Goblin Market* like a pamphlet from a shoe,

said the elements would damage and ferment us,

I heard its motile feet damp the rusting ground,

quinces and greengages smash like cuttle waves,

I trusted there was this way and only this,

you understand why on the snaky path to knowledge,

a charmer in a mossy glen, cloyed with fruit gnashed from

sisters' necks, she sprang from the velvet nap of it,

and I ahead to the edge, a patchwork of tears

and kneaded breads, a poster for *désastre* and *ruine*,

important parapets to walk,

I dillied to its dally, some of it blistered me,

it was modeling a good bit and craning

so that it came down to what it always does:

what did more, adoration or flogging,

Its zeitgeist gone, it struggled to *ten-hut*, it dribbled

the afterbirth of joy, the look of it sanguine,

abloom in a brotherhood of winks and nods,

Angela Vogel

I plied it like Narcissus, like a joker sent to penetrate a club,

sweet maroon sumac skirting us, haloed,

waltzing like sugary fire, somewhere off suffering

& singing in a featherless sleep, a manoeuvre

both manly and over.

## Legitimacy Is So Chummy

First thing is: everyone presses the room.

To handshake the perimeter

like a grass snake: the clammy waiting

to get their chance at you.

Go on handyswipe boy. Give them a little wink.

Listen: you tell them what you want.

You get it and you are kind.

Maybe everyone wins the big contract.

Maybe we could all be the stockholders.

What do you say?  Calluses only show

on the outside.  You're one

of those guys, never built a muscle

but pillowy hands.

Say, *hello.*

Say, *Let's do business.*

I've always loved you

like a wallet, you know.

J. P. Dancing Bear

## *Magic, Isn't It*

You, the imp among the light sockets.

All block-eyed and torquing a spell

of ozone. Scroll of carpet rot . . .

an *I curse thee*... Love as eye

of newt or bat wing—or wiggly thing

mixed into the bigger cauldron.

O black cat, o matted wanderer,

evil never walks into a room

but is waiting for the interviewer

to ask him the question he's always wanted

# J. P. Dancing Bear

to answer.  There is so much fading

to black.  God rolled a twenty-sided dice

once—then all hell broke loose.

You were thinking of going back to sawing

young assistants in half—

not nearly the sticky mess on your karma—

it's less trouble, really, and the pay's much better.

## J. P. Dancing Bear

### *Deadline World*

This way every minute is the last.

I jammed my thumb shoving paper in

the printer, pressed the key,

let it fly with one eye on the ticking time.

Someone quotes the love of adrenaline

but I don't know—love, proper love, takes

time. Now a voice over

the cube wall says, *better to have loved*

*and lost than never to have...* the loser.

I overhear the quote about wages

not keeping up with the cost of living,

and then I cannot remember

what milk tastes like.

I think it must be thick and flabby

and it might be sweet, because...

why else?

Someone's radio reports

that siphoning from tanks

and driving away without paying

at the pump have increased

## J. P. Dancing Bear

at alarming rates.

Alarm bells—I think it all began there

with the dual-function alarm bell that marked

panic and signaled the next class all in one.

I had to run the length of school

not to be tardy. I had all the state-issued books

on my back. Out of breath and sliding

into a chair at the bell.

The clock resets itself every hour,

you know. Just now, I'm three minutes

into the next deadline.

Dorianne Laux

## *Dog Moon*

The old dog next door won't stop barking

at the moon. My neighbor is keeping a log:

what time, how long, if howling is involved.

I know she's awake as I am, robe askew,

calling animal control, while I drink dark tea

and stare out my window at the Voodoo moon,

throwing beads of light into the arms

of the bare-chested trees. Who can blame him

when the moon is as big as a kitchen clock,

ticking like a time bomb? The bright full moon

with its beryl core and striated face, its plasma umbra,

pouring borrowed light into every abyss on earth,

turning the rivers silver, plowing the mountains'

shadows across grasslands and deserts, towns

riddled with mineshafts, oil rigs and mills,

yellow tractors asleep in the untilled fields.

The what-were-they-like-moon staring down

on rain-pocked gravestones, worming its way

into gopher holes, setting barbed wire fences ablaze.

Who wouldn't love this old tooth moon,

# Dorianne Laux

this toilet paper moon, this feral, flea-bitten moon

is his moon, too. Certain-of-nothing moon, bone

he can't wait to sink his teeth into. Radio moon,

the white dial tuned to static. Panic moon,

pulling a cloud like a blanket over its baby face.

Moon a portrait hung from a nail

in the starred hallway of the past.

Full moon that won't last.

I can hear that dog clawing at the fence.

Moon a manhole cover sunk in the boulevard

of night, monocle on a chain, well of light,

a frozen pond lifted and thrown like a discus

onto the sky. I scratch my skull, look down

into my stained empty cup. That dog

has one blind eye, the other's looking up.

Lee Upton

## *Dear Succubus*

Ornery and ancient

enemy of happiness,

does it alarm you

that at last I can see how you've grown:

your barnacled

tree stump,

your florid hump,

your half pints of bitters

bitterly cresting me.

I don't understand what

you've been saving up.

How warm is my body?

Aren't there warmer bodies?

Have you always been with me?

(I think so). And if so,

when will my blood

turn the tide of yours?

When will you become

what I would have become?

When do I get to pummel

# Lee Upton

your lungs and crouch

like a toad on your chest?

Or, more likely, when you're nearly done with me,

when do I float free, whittled

into near-air, thin as thistledown—

and if so, remember:

thistledown, so unlike its father,

thistledown, that little fuse.

Lesley Wheeler

## The Unbeliever Takes a Hike

Winter is a cracked path, all the plush of moss

and needles, mulch and soil swept away

by the god of water. I have no choice

but to sit down or follow it, so I follow, day

after heathen day, sometimes watching my feet

lest I trip on an exposed blade of shale,

usually muttering, indiscreet,

since no one is listening. Once in a while

the sheen on the creek will interrupt

my monologue, its coppery greens will spill

into the air and I remember about

the world. Its shadows crowd, its leaves fall

with no display of self-regard, no doubt

that spring will come again with crocus,

clouds, and frilly tender feelings. Devout

# Lesley Wheeler

branches pray their red beads with breezy hocus-

pocus: they believe in the slanting sun, its power

to bring them to life when it wishes. So, I focus:

I can at least believe in looking. I stare

over the bank's edge, where the burble has skin

like a cold pudding, and see filigreed feathers,

ice shaped like a dove, like some spirit-sign,

where two bare branches dangle in a cross.

Chills. All this nature a prank to take me in.

Judith Harris

## A Study of Ted Kooser's "Etude"

"Etude," which is the French word for "Study," is the opening poem in Ted Kooser's 1994 book, *Weather Central* (Pitt). "Etude," not unlike Stevens' "Study of Two Pears," captures the still life not merely as a representation of reality but as a metaphor for reality—or how we come to conceptualize our world through figuration. Metaphor is born out of the implicit and the explicit realms of the mind mirrored in nature and nature mirrored in the mind. Metaphor is also the poet's paintbrush as it settles objects compositionally. As Kooser comments on "Etude":

> Of my poems of metaphor, and there are so many, this one is perhaps the one that leaps the furthest and makes the most distant (and perhaps peculiar) connections. I use it with students sometimes to show how once the metaphor has taken flight it must at last be brought back to ground. In that poem it happens with the phrase "like the beak of a bird." (from an email exchange with the author)

Here, Kooser suggests that metaphor, with all its resilience, is always appetitive, always taking us into its parallel universe and asking us to willingly suspend our disbelief that such a world could exist. But metaphor has a way of not only telling the truth, but telling it more truly. For example, Williams' "To Waken an Old Lady" is a poem that gets lost in the figurative terms of its own inducement and then arrives back to the literal more literally than anything real could express. It begins: "Old age is /a flight of small /cheeping birds" and then, through following the birds' behaviors (gaining and buffeting, then resting on the seed covered snow), reveals more profound meanings of old age and its varied gratifications. As we read further, we discover that the snow and wind have covered the barren landscape with seeds and seed husks, suggesting that old age is similarly covered with sustenance. The birds' vibrant activity brings to light a surprising connection between fertility and old age.

But what is a metaphor? The root "meta" means change or involving change, between or backward—and "phor" derives from "to bear" or to labor, carry, or create. Hence metaphor implies an action of mind in which one term or concept is carried or conveyed into another in order to create a new and synthesized concept. Implicit in this process is the bearing or birth-formation of something vital and fresh in place of something in language that has become deadened or mordant.

In the Romantic era, a transformative period in human consciousness and aesthetics, poems were seen as organically metaphorical in such a way that each metaphor is organically related to the poem as flowers to a plant. The ideal model of the poem as an intricate form involves all the relationships of its elements to one another, not a decorative surface of figurations meant to embellish the poem's surface.

The Modernist idea of metaphor revolves around the notion that when an artist achieves a semblance in a work, the work seems to articulate a profound emotion on its own without reference to its creator. It has become sufficiently autonomous. Pound saw the framework of the metaphor as a kind of darting in and out of consciousness and association. Thus, instead of defining the metaphor as Burns might have centuries before: "my love is like a red, red rose"(in which the rose stands for love, a 'this is for that' representation), modern and postmodern adaptations of metaphor suggest an interactive dynamic that is always circling between and through the contraries of two terms: a 'this into that' representation. With this explanation in the background, we can see why Kooser emphasizes metaphor as central to his art.

# ETUDE

I have been watching a Great Blue Heron
fish in the cattails, easing ahead
with the stealth of a lover composing a letter,
the hungry words looping and blue
as they coil and uncoil, as they kiss and sting.

Let's say that he holds down an everyday job
in an office. His blue suit blends in.
Long days swim beneath the glass top
of his desk, each one alike. On the tip
of each morning, a bubble trembles.

No one has seen him there, writing a letter
to a woman he loves. His pencil is poised
in the air like the beak of a bird.
He would spear the whole world if he could,
toss it and swallow it live.

    The poem opens by situating us in the traditional setting of the poet in nature, observing the landscape, something insentient, but using his own sentience to translate it into a human language that has meaning.  This meaning is then communicated to the reader who revives the scene in his or her own mind, making the poem a correspondent to the living world it creates and disassembles. Because postmodernism has validated synchronicity, it has also allowed the contemporary poet to place more distance between the literal term and the figurative term, juxtaposing them in a way that renders a simultaneous reading of overlapping and multiple realms of experience, rather than persuading us of the veracity of only one. Thus the poem is allowed to act on two or more surfaces.  The still life, ordinarily still, becomes a study in motion.

    Thus the poem of metaphor, as Kooser might describe it, does not provide ready answers to the reader's questions about his reference world, but it does supply a relationship between two things that appear to be incompatible. What is true for the poet becomes true for the reader. When Kooser comments that this kind of poem is the poem he had been trying to write, it suggests a breakthrough: a poem that has succeeded in completing itself. Despite its divisions into smaller fractions (each stanza has a different context), the poem has brought itself back into a unitary, living whole.

Subsequently, in the first stanza, we learn major things about the speaker, context, and condition. We learn that the speaker comes upon the Great Blue Heron he's been watching as a singular fish is caught in predatory cattails. We learn something else about the Heron's agility: "he is easing ahead / with the stealth of a lover composing a letter." This is the poet's first launch of the Heron; we know that the words, like the cattails that seem to entrap Kooser, are not unlike the emotions that a lover has in writing a letter—that may woo the beloved with the sting of longing; hence, "they kiss and sting." But they are enmeshed, and not yet sorted out for meaning.

Stanza two addresses the reader directly, offering an interpretation of the speaker's own interpretation, an analogy for the already analogized. "Let's say" that this Blue Heron holds down a job in an office, where he blends in with everyone else and where, we may infer, it uses correspondence as a means of moving through time, but dispassionate writing, writing that is dictated, or copied, and has no real life or appeal to it. This seems credible enough as a further imitation of the original Heron caught in the stream: both the office worker and the Heron sit above the reflective surface of the desk or the water; each of them does that every morning, and each morning something like a bubble is about to explode or pop; then it will be over—what was ever gained will be lost again in the flux. Furthermore, on the tip of each morning, there is the possibility of the undercurrent of the poet's suppressed imagination bursting into reality-literally speaking, coming up for air. The speaker, then, tries to find some balance between the world above and the world below.

In stanza three, we find ourselves in a new atmosphere, a new dislocation. We've moved from the stream, to the office of the businessman, and now to the world of the observer. But no one has seen him there, writing a letter. Now we are poised in the air and looking down. The composition process is a matter of nominating words, "spearing" them out of the flux of all other words. A word is significant because it is different: and so is the poet in the act of composing inside the businessman's suit. As the fantasy and the reality reverse, we realize that the wooden beak is really a pencil! We are inside, not outside, the mind of the poet. What drives the pencil to pierce the sky with a word? The poet's hunger: his hunger for direct experience, passion, for entry into life—wild life, outside the monotony of the office.

In the last stanza, we have "lost" hold of the Blue Heron. The air is the new yet unwritten page of life—in which anything can happen. It is here that the speaker offers up his lustful fantasy of using his pencil to spear not only the Blue Heron but also the entire world. Dissatisfied with a language that puts words into cages of business correspondence to be consumed, he acts, to spare them. And the only way to spare them is to hide them by swallowing them back. In the end, there is some diffidence in the last line: how does one "toss it" and at the same time swallow it alive? Is he discarding the object of his desire or his pursuit of it? If he could consume the whole world, he would, to let others consume it. There is a tone of absolute exuberance in that last line, which conveys just what it says: "alive." In our own way, we, as readers, are all the recipients of this love letter.

Tony Leuzzi

## By Way of Play and Accident:
## An Interview with Karen Volkman

The following discussion took place on May 09, 2008, at Housing Works Bookstore in New York City. At the time, Karen Volkman's new sonnet sequence, Nomina, had just been released by BOA Editions, LTD. As many critics have already realized, Nomina is a tour de force of formal innovation, a brilliant synthesis of the Italian sonnet with the dense, swirling verbal textures of Hopkins, Rilke, and the French symbolists. Given her vast intellectual powers, Volkman's considerations of her poetry—and of poetry in general—are as rigorous and satisfying as the poems themselves.

**TL: Let's start with a broad question: what intellectual and emotional impulses inspired you to write this sonnet sequence?**

**KV:** The sonnets came about in the best way—through play and accident. I anticipated going in the direction of a more spacious mode after the density and compression of the Spar poems, thinking in terms of a long poem or serial poem. Then I started reading sonnets in preparation for a forms class I was scheduled to teach. And not just English language sonnets. I'd just spent a stretch of time in Germany, and my German had developed enough for me to read Rilke's Sonnets to Orpheus in the original. These were poems that had been very important to me in translation, and experiencing them as formal sonnets was a shock. First, I experienced them as sound-structures in a very immediate way—with a foreign language, especially one you're new to, there is always a momentary disconnect between registering sound and meaning, so the material quality comes through more palpably. And second, I realized that this very subtle, complex thinking could be done in such a strict, constrained form. It was like rediscovering another character of poems that had been important to me through my whole writing life. I was moved by this to look at Mallarme's sonnets in French (my French was good at that point, and there were many poets I read in the original, but I'd always been daunted by Mallarme's difficulty). His brilliant, saturated musicality was a complete revelation. Again, the slight remove from the language made it even more purely an aural experience. Sound was so important a concern in Spar, and here I was experiencing it on a whole new level. I thought, "I want to make a poem that sounds like that. A wall of sound, totally overwhelming." I tried a few, and ended up writing about twenty in the first month, a number of which are in *Nomina*.

**TL: Why the Italian sonnet form over the English?**

**KV:** Largely, it was the greater constraints that the form imposes, a greater suffering (laughs), the awareness of that greater constraint, and the sheer sensuousness of the sound and musicality, that wall-of-sound effect, where you feel almost assaulted and overwhelmed by the recurrence of rhymes. In the Shakespearean sonnet form there is a more varied music, whereas I wanted the sounds of the poems to be engulfing.

**TL: I sense some of this engulfing you speak of comes about not only through the repetition of sounds but the way you build phrases, through a series of enumerations that are hypnotic. As a result, something beyond conventional meaning is being communicated through the sounds.**

**KV:** Yes, a frenetic quality, the way matter keeps happening, keeps mutating, the pushing of matter into different shapes. The material world is in constant motion, constant, compulsive making and changing. When I was writing these poems I was thinking of constant motion and activity in the cosmos and in the elements around us, and wanted to make the furious activity of a material intelligence felt in the materiality and movement of the poems.

**TL: In poems 58-61, I saw an illuminating contrast between the building up into a whole or striving towards a whole and the dismantling of the whole, its destruction, its breaking down. For example, the stitching and splitting references in the poem "See the crack at the quick of the accident." There is a persistent idea of rupture and**

the scar and the "stitched divisibles." Thus, contrary energies seem to be at work, where there is an attempt to bring things together and split them apart.

KV: Well, that seems to me to be a central schism in the sonnet itself and why I find it such a compelling, compulsive and fascinating form to work with. There is a presumed resolution in the fixed rhyme scheme, so the regularity of pattern presents the sound structure under the sign of rationality and control. But that premise is contradicted by the nature of sound itself—once you're in the realm of sound association, there's a constant proliferation that's possible, which isn't fixed to the meaning of words. Once the form calls attention to the word as a unit of sound, the word seems to push against its own semantic boundaries. It almost seems to perceive itself as sound and be having a crisis.

On various levels the notion of both breaking open and the fixing in place are operative in the sonnet, particularly in its formal imperatives—but it's also in the language. We have charged fields of sound and the sounds are always pushing against the boundaries of words, and the idea of betraying the freedom of sound by putting the borders of particular reference on them is a kind of violence. We're trapped within a linguistic system of having our perceptions structured—on a deep level we experience the contradiction of wanting openness and needing a certain amount of closure in order to communicate.

TL: You've explored this theme in your other books, too…

KV: Yes. The sonnet is a different way of staging the argument and seeing how this tradition points to very deep contradictions framed in a particular set of terms.

TL: Many of the sonnets in *Nomina* are beaded throughout with what would seem like specialized vocabulary for the average reader.

KV: Some words I found in the dictionary. "Integral" is a word that comes up in earlier poems of mine. Words fascinate me, not only by their sounds but the fields of reference that they open, the associations, the way they seem charged.

TL: In what way do you think "integral" is charged?

KV: To me, it conveys the idea of an essence, something pulling into itself—the charge is spatial in terms of the sensation of something compressed and tense with a quality that is held within but outwardly expressed. I get a feeling of a semantic space or motion being opened up by it.

TL: Some of the poems have that feel, too, a kind of compression. Some of the poems deal well with the concept of ellipsis. In fact, the poems themselves are elliptical, brief snatches of sense or meaning that are deliberately—for whatever reason—cut off or withheld or never realized...for example, on page 25: "This ellipse...slip between seasons." I feel, in many ways, this statement is a kind of poetics for the book. Would you agree with that?

KV: Well it certainly could be. I think there are a lot of places in the book that could be propositions for a poetics, taken on, shifted or turned around. Here, it is the idea of the ellipse and slippages between any certain positive meaning.

TL: I admire your ability to choose words that are connotatively and denotatively rich, even elastic. The word "crux," for example, has a number of definitions, all of which are simultaneously possible in the poem "Yet, through. No one speaking, no one moves." Even better are the multi-referential potential of words such as "occluded," "efferent," "apsis," "radix" and "lumen" in the poem "Blank bride of the hour, occluded thought." How do you consider your word choices in any given poem?

KV: "Efferent," "apsis," and "radix" are all words I happened on in the dictionary. It's kind of a mystery how wandering into a certain word-field seems to create a magnetic attraction to other words—or how a particular word's field seems to draw others into it. Partly it's a matter of sound, but there is something else going on too. Several of the poets who most intrigue me have a certain near-fetishistic attachment to a lexicon that seems transformed by their attentions—Dickinson, with "circumference," Hopkins with "dapple."

**TL: What stays with me even after several reads is the mathematical imagery in the book. In a poem like "Never ..." I was blown away by the play on the words "integral skin," "cardinal animal" "ordinal net": integral, cardinal and ordinal each have several associations, all of which are working simultaneously in the poem. And yet you said you composed these rather quickly, so was most of the work done before the writing—did you research words beforehand?**

KV: Most of them came spontaneously without planning beforehand. There is far more spontaneity than study—the sonnets were mostly written very quickly, and the "sound chains" are basically musical improvisations. Getting into that space could take some doing, though, which is why there were often long lag periods between bursts of writing. And then there were many discarded poems that had a sonic cohesion, but were lacking in other qualities—that seemed merely formulaic. The fifty that are in the book are the most successful results of the diabolical experiment. I liked "Cardinal" and "Ordinal" they have mathematical and sound associations.

**TL: Christian ones, too...**

KV: Being Jewish, I don't think much about that (laughs). I'm never entirely sure why I'm drawn to mathematical language because I'm not at all mathematical.

**TL Do you see yourself as a Jewish writer participating in that great tradition of Jewish writers?**

KV: I haven't been a practicing Jew for many years, but I identify culturally as Jewish. I grew up going to synagogue—depending on how faithful my parents were feeling at the time (laughs)—and we belonged to a conservative congregation, with services in Hebrew. It was strange to grow up hearing a language you're aware of as sacred, but don't understand—so the idea of holiness is bound up with the incomprehensible, a mysterious and coded speech. I remember experiencing these services as deeply sad, with the words often chanted or half-sung. My sense of sound as evoking mysteries and powers beyond the referential boundaries of language started with those services. I studied the songs in Hebrew school and looking at the letters on the page. Moreover, the mythology of wandering in the desert, of being dispossessed, the exodus, are foundational ideas in my work.

**TL: I wonder if that might have something to do with the fact that many of your poems are concerned with closing gaps, and attempt to achieve wholeness.**

**KV:** In my books, there is a constant awareness of, if not a divine force, a large annihilating force that's out there and can destroy at any time. The Hebrew God is a very dangerous god—very temperamental, very destructive.

**TL: At the same time, the Hebrew God frequently gives his people, not only second chances, but third, fourth, and fifth ones…He can be alternately terrifying and forgiving.**

**KV:** Yes, he's completely unpredictable. You never know what's going to happen. He can be benevolent but he can throw a serious temper tantrum. The Lot's Wife tale was particularly horrifying to me when I was a kid. I remember reading an illustrated book of bible stories for children and seeing an image of a pillar of salt, knowing it was once a woman—and it was horrifying, and uncanny. Why, of all possible punishments, a pillar of salt?

**TL: I read a fine review of** *Nomina* **in** *The National Poetry Review.* **The author had insightful things to say about your work—particularly in regards to Mallarme's influence on your work. But what struck me**

most was the writer's qualifiers. I came across phrases like "seems telling," "at the very least one feels," "could be," and "whatever the case," as if certainty with regards to your work were impossible.

**KV:** That writer, Douglas Basford, had the manuscript of *Nomina*, but was in fact specifically asked by the journal to explicate two sonnets, "Nice knuckle, uncle" and "That's what it says to the bloomingest more." He may have felt more bound to attempt precise "readings" of lines for that reason, which is no easy feat for these poems. I think his comments overall and especially broader observations on the book and currents in my work are quite brilliant. Comments on any difficult poetry are bound to require a lot of qualifiers—I seem frequently to say to my students, when we're talking about this or that line of, say, Dickinson, that I've been thinking about it for years and am still not sure what to make of it. A student just last week pointed out what a strange line is Stevens' "a body wholly body, fluttering its empty sleeves." I hope my readers will accept the experience of feeling like strangers in a strange land when they enter the poems, and not feel too bound to parse them, or abashed if they're not sure what every phrase means. Being lost is a feeling I personally enjoy, in a city or in a poem. The great thing about the sonnet is that a reader can't get too lost, because the form itself is familiar and provides a frame and orientation on a sound level.

**TL:** As challenging as your poems are, they invite the reader to become intimate with them in ways I rarely see in the contemporary poem. I found myself working so hard at each poem that later, when I turned to another writer's work, that work seemed bland, shallow. Your work requires a good deal of commitment, but the pay off is enormous.

**KV:** Here too, I don't think of it as work, but pleasure and play. Even with the most difficult poets, I just don't feel the engagement is "work." Reading Mallarme isn't working, it's traveling, or it's being projected into peculiar spaces and states, or hearing sounds in your mind that create such an intelligent pattern, you feel your relationship to sound and word has entirely shifted. As far as "commitment," I don't ask readers to commit to anything but having an unusual experience—hopefully different than they've ever had before, hopefully pleasurable and strange, but not laborious! Intimacy is an interesting term to raise given the poems' "impersonality" and frequent lack of an "I." This too may be partly due to the familiarity of the sonnet form and the immediate connection that sound invites. It establishes a sensory relationship and allure that is "immediate" in that it doesn't require the mediation of sense; it skips past the meaning-making impulse straight to the pleasure of musical pattern.

**TL: You've admitted the influence of Mallarme on your work. Could you expand on this?**

**KV:** His series of four sonnets called Plusieurs Sonnets were really pivotal. The density of language and sound, and the way he revolves certain images: the constellation, the empty room, mirrors, hair.... some near fetishistic images that reoccur throughout his poems. Also, too, the ambiguity of syntax. All of this plays into how I conceived my sonnets. This seemingly closed form, under the pressure of Mallarme's brilliant poetic compulsions, is constantly fragmented by ambiguous syntax, so at nearly any point in these sonnets there could be multiple meanings and readings to his phrases and clauses.

**TL: One of the most arresting sonnets for me is the working with the Orphic myth, such as the throat-flute sonnet. Want to talk about this poem?**

**KV:** This was one of the earlier sonnets. Some of the terms we see later in the book, such as the "claim," the idea of wakefulness and being aware and attuned, the sameness, which comes up in other poems, a lot of optimistic claims being made…Various propositions are made in the book, questioned and then turned around, seen in darker lights and sometimes more optimistic lights. This poem balances both the dark and light and makes some propositions about the "never same"… the "throat flute" is that utterance and audibility and articulation of a momentary self of language, which has so many possibilities…but in the end there is also so much anxiety about the possibility of failure: is this expression the magic of the ability to express and articulate, what happens when it is received? That's where the anxiety comes in.

**TL: Do you think some of the earlier poems, such as this one, determined or set forward the language that comes through in the later poems?**

KV: Yes, to some extent, though some of the later poems brought in new terms.

**TL: I was wondering if you might give a close reading of two of your poems, the pair that begin "I asked every flower," which I feel are among the finest in the collection. Would you be willing to walk through each one, explaining not only what they mean to you, but perhaps some of the considerations that went into their construction?**

KV: The opening two lines "I asked every flower I met/had they seen my palest friend" come from a situation in a chapter of the Hans Christian Andersen tale "The Snow Queen," which has been important to me all my life. The little boy Kay falls under the spell of the evil queen and is taken off to her icy palace. His friend Gerda sets off to find him and has various adventures. At one point, she wanders through a garden asking the different flowers if they've seen him. But the flowers are lost in their own meditations and only tell her their strange flower story — apart from roses, which are kind enough to report that they were underground and did not see Kay's corpse. Otherwise, the question isn't really responded to, so the speaker here gets more of a reply than poor little Gerda, though not particularly consoling ones. The speaker is a bereft Orphic wanderer in search of the lost beloved – and gets the bad news that the world doesn't care. Not only that, but "to search is only to same," so even the act of seeking is questioned. The desire for possession and location of a beloved might be just injury and distortion. A quote by Simone Weil that I've always found terrifying is "The 'I' leaves its mark on the world as it destroys." The implications for a lyric speaker are devastating. The poems are two of the earliest of the tetrameter sonnets in the book, at a point where I'd written many pentameter pieces and wanted to have a different sense of weight and movement, a lighter, more song-like quality, which seemed right for the fragility and strangeness of the "conversation." And the rhymes of course are the same in both, indicating how circumscribed the terms are, how repetitive the quest. I intended there to be a third poem using the same rhymes, but never could finish it.

TL: In the second of the two poems that begin "I asked every flower I met" you conclude, "To search is only to same." In many ways this encapsulates the themes of the book, that the act of naming something is perhaps to shape that thing in a way we already understand, or shape it so that we can understand it.

KV: There's definitely that anxiety in the claim. To seek something out and name it—is that a way to arrest it and therefore limit its meaning? In a kinder light it could be seen as a form of devotion or as a desire to encompass the expressive energy of the thing being named, to bound it.

TL: But the notion of search is twofold: we search for things we've lost or we search for things we do not yet possess. Yet both of these notions would seem to be undercut by "same," which suggests that we're searching for something we already know...

KV: In this particular poem, the flower is addressing the speaker's sorrow in searching for the beloved, the "palest friend." This beloved is a specific being who has been lost. However, it could be an unknown, a concept, or some object of desire that is undiscovered. So yes, there is a suggestion that the desire that leads to the searching is a reflexive desire to see what you have already seen or to have your memories reaffirmed.

TL: You do tend to make universal statements in these poems. For example, in the poem "She goes, she is, she wakes the waters" the line "Her hands hold many or her hands hold none." To me there is, once again, that tension between wholeness and emptiness, presence and absence." Furthermore, there is only the choice between two extremes: many or none. Why not "some" or "a few"?

KV: I think the sonnet is an extreme form that I've tried to push to its extreme limits in Nomina. And the poets who have most influenced me with regards to this form are poets of extremes, such as Mallarme, who created incredibly dense sound structures in his sonnets, trying to push towards an extreme intensity—the words have these insights on the nature of the material on the expressivity—those occasions of intensity and extremity were the ones that seemed to charge me in the writing of my sonnets.

TL: That is true of Hopkins, too. And like Hopkins you tend to employ the technique of enallage, recasting words in different parts of speech, such as making a noun into a verb.

KV: Also in Hopkins even the smallest thing being observed became the center of the world; his meditative energies tend to charge the language, an intense awareness of expressivity.

TL: The book is impeccably arranged. Did you compose these poems in tandem or did you write them and arrange them in a new order?

KV: They were arranged this way after they were written.

TL: In the final line of *Nomina* you write, "the bride is fled." Not has fled, but is fled. One prevailing conceit of sonnet sequences is the idea of coming together, of unity that is achieved despite physical separation. Here, however, the final image is flight.

KV: And yet, another conceit of the sonnet is that the beloved is always out of reach. And even in Shakespeare's sonnets, the lover cannot always control the beloved; resolution and "mastery" of form is only apparent; the beloved can't be contained, as the word can't fully control its sounds. Of my three books, that line is the one ending I'm happy with, because I felt the other two books gave in to the longing for a firmer resolve. But flight and distance seems truer to the experience of poetry—always wanting. The energies of the sonnet often try to exceed its frame, just as the bride herself flees out of the frame of the sequence and the boundaries that are being put on her, including her categorization as "bride."

**TL: And yet it's not total escape because, as you write in that same poem, there is an "endless loop." She has fled, but presumably into some other frame...**

**KV:** Yes, she is an elusive energy that is always trying to be pinned down. As a "bride" she is open and receptive to a degree; part of her aspect is a desire to marry, engage with experience, but she doesn't want to be contained in this structure.

# Notes on the Authors

**Jeannette Allée**'s work has appeared in *The Best American Poetry 2007, The Iowa Review, FIELD, Fence,* and *Gulf Coast*. She is a recipient of a 4Culture grant and an Artist Trust grant.

**Cindy Beebe** lives in Collierville, Tennessee, near Memphis, where she works with at-risk children and youth. Her poems have appeared, or are forthcoming, in several journals, including *The Southern Review, The Midwest Quarterly, Rock & Sling, The Sow's Ear Poetry Review,* and *Grasslimb*.

**Ben Berman** won the 2002 Erika Mumford Prize from the New England Poetry Club and is a recipient of a 2008 Poetry Fellowship from the Massachusetts Cultural Council. He has poems published in *Salamander, Burnside Review, The Cimarron Review, Cream City Review, Cutthroat Journal, The Connecticut Review* and others.

**Sarah Blackman** received her MFA in fiction from the University of Alabama where she currently teaches literature and creative writing. Her most recent poetry has appeared or is forthcoming in *Third Coast, santa clara review* and *Court Green*.

**Sam Byfield** is the author of *From the Middle Kingdom* (Pudding House Press). He has been published or is forthcoming in *Meridian, Diner,* and the 2008 *Outside Voices* anthology (North America), *Heat* and *LiNQ* (Australia), and extensively online. He currently works for a public health/environment NGO in southwest China.

**Patrick Carrington** is the author of *Hard Blessings* (MSR Publishing, 2008), *Thirst* (Codhill, 2007), and *Rise, Fall and Acceptance* (MSR Publishing, 2006). His poems are forthcoming in *West Branch, The Bellingham Review, American Literary Review, Bellevue Literary Review,* and elsewhere. He teaches creative writing in New Jersey and serves as the poetry editor of *Mannequin Envy*.

**Mark Conway**'s book *Any Holy City* won the Gerald Cable Award. This poem is from a manuscript entitled *Dreaming Man, Face Down*; other poems from the ms. have appeared or will appear in the *American Poetry Review, Slate, the Alaska Quarterly Review* and other journals.

**T. Zachary Cotler** has published in *Paris Review, Southern Review, Denver Quarterly, Barrow Street, Massachusetts Review* and *Witness*. He was the 2006 Amy Clampitt Fellow.

**J. P. Dancing Bear** 's poems have apeared in *Shenandoah, Mississippi Review, Natural Bridge, Cimarron Review, Poetry East, North American Review, Verse Daily, The National Poetry Review, Poetry International, Marlboro Review, Cranky,* et cetera. His next book, *Inner Cities of Gulls,* will be published by Salmon Poetry in 2010. He edits *The American Poetry Journal*.

**Oliver de la Paz** is the author of two collections of poetry, *Names Above Houses,* and *Furious*

*Lullaby*, both published by Southern Illinois University Press. His work has appeared in journals such as *The Virginia Quarterly Review, North American Review*, and elsewhere. He teaches creative writing at Western Washington University.

**Teresa Chuc Dowell** has a B.A. in Philosophy. Her poems have appeared in or are forthcoming in print and online magazines including *Community Life Magazine, Jack Magazine, PoetryMagazine.com, and Miller's Pond*. Her short stories have appeared in or are forthcoming in print and online magazines including *SugarMule.com* and *Memoir (and)*. Teresa teaches English literature at a Los Angeles public high school.

**Angie Estes'** fourth collection of poetry, *Tryst*, will be published by Oberlin College Press in 2009. Her awards include a Pushcart Prize, a National Endowment for the Arts Fellowship in Poetry, and the Alice Fay di Castagnola Prize from the Poetry Society of America.

**Judith Harris** is the author of two poetry collections from LSU Press: *Atonement* (2000) and *The Bad Secret* (2003) and a critical book on poetry and psychoanalysis, S*ignifying Pain: Constructing and Healing the Self through Writing* (SUNY Press, 2003). Poems have been published by *Slate, The American Scholar, Boulevard, The Southern Review, Antioch Review, Ploughshares, Prairie Schooner, Poetry Northwest, Margie*, and *Cincinnati Review*, and "American Life in Poetry," Ted Kooser's syndicated newspaper column.

**Dyani Johns** is a PhD student in the English department at the University of California, Davis where she is studying renaissance literature, Latin American poetry and translation. She is currently working on her first book of poems.

A finalist for the National Book Critics Circle Award, **Dorianne Laux**'s fourth book of poems, *Facts about the Moon* (W.W. Norton), is the recipient of the Oregon Book Award and was short-listed for the Lenore Marshall Poetry Prize. Laux is also author of *Awake* (1990) *What We Carry* (1994) *Smoke* (2000) and *Superman: The Chapbook* (2008). She and her husband, poet Joseph Millar, recently moved to Raleigh where she joins the faculty at North Carolina State University.

**Tony Leuzzi**'s poems and prose appear in *Pinyon, California Quarterly, Arts and Letters, Sentence, SLANT, The Harvard Educational Review*, et cetera. His first book of poems, *Tongue-Tied and Singing*, was published by Foothills Press in 2004.

**Beth Martinelli**'s work has appeared in journals such as *Southern Poetry Review, Pleiades, Barrow Street* and *The Threepenny Review*, among others. She recently served as the 2006 Philip Roth Resident in Creative Writing at Bucknell University's Stadler Center for Poetry. Her chapbook, *To Darkness*, is from Finishing Line Press

**Darren Morris** is a graduate of the MFA program at Virginia Commonwealth University. His poems have appeared in *The American Poetry Review, River Styx, Rattle*, the Meridian Press anthology *Best New Poets 2008*, and others. His fiction has been awarded a fellowship from The Virginia Commission for the Arts.

**Amit Majmudar** is a Diagnostic Radiologist completing a Nuclear Medicine fellowship in Cleveland, Ohio, where he lives with his wife and twin sons. His first book will be published by TriQuarterly Books / Northwestern University Press.

**Mia Nussbaum**'s writing has appeared recently in, or is forthcoming from, *Greatcoat, the Iowa Review, the Beloit Poetry Journal, the New Orleans Review* and *Commonweal*. She lives in Colorado.

**Rita Mae Reese** has received a Rona Jaffe Foundation Writers' Award, a Stegner fellowship, and a "Discovery"/The Nation award. Her work has appeared in *32 Poems, Bloom, The Southern Review, The Nation, Prairie Schooner,* and *From Where You Dream*. She lives with her wife and daughter in San Francisco.

**Melissa Stein**'s poems have appeared in *Southern Review, American Poetry Review, New England Review, Gulf Coast, Indiana Review, The Journal,* and many other journals and anthologies. A freelance writer and editor in San Francisco, she holds an MA in creative writing from the University of California at Davis.

**Angela Vogel**'s poems have appeared in *POOL, Barrow Street, Southern Poetry Review, Valparaiso Poetry Review, RHINO, GoodFoot,* & *Folio*. She is a 2004 Pushcart Prize nominee, and her chapbook, *Social Smile,* was published in 2004 by Finishing Line Press. She holds a MFA from the University of Maryland at College Park and received a Maryland Arts Council Fellowship. She teaches Poetry & Women's Studies and publishes *New Zoo Poetry Review*.

**Lesley Wheeler** holds an Individual Artist Fellowship from the Virginia Commission for the Arts. Her poems appear in *Poetry, AGNI, Witness,* and other journals, and in the chapbook *Scholarship Girl*; her second scholarly book, *Voicing American Poetry,* was just published by Cornell University Press. She teaches at Washington and Lee University in Lexington, Virginia.

**Martha Zweig**'s *Monkey Lightning,* her third full-length collection, will appear from Tupelo Press in 2009. *Vinegar Bone* (1999) and *What Kind* (2003), are published by Wesleyan University Press. Powers, from the Vermont Council on the Arts is her chapbook. Zweig's poetry has received a Whiting Award and has appeared recently or is forthcoming in *The Progressive, Ploughshares, Pequod, Boston Review, The Paris Review, Poetry Daily,* and *Verse Daily*.

**Lee Upton** is the author of five books of poems, most recently *Undid in the Land of Undone,* and four books of literary criticism. Her novella, *The Guide to the Flying Island,* won the Miami University Novella Contest and will be published by Miami in 2009.

www.ingramcontent.com/pod-product-compliance
Lightning Source LLC
Chambersburg PA
CBHW031408040426
42444CB00005B/473